D1518719

# Zoom In on
# Powerful Machines

# Trucks

Andrea Rivera

**abdopublishing.com**

Published by Abdo Zoom™, PO Box 398166, Minneapolis, Minnesota 55439. Copyright © 2017 by
Abdo Consulting Group, Inc. International copyrights reserved in all countries. No part of this book may be
reproduced in any form without written permission from the publisher. Abdo Zoom™ is a trademark and logo
of Abdo Consulting Group, Inc.

Printed in the United States of America, North Mankato, Minnesota
102016
012017

THIS BOOK CONTAINS
RECYCLED MATERIALS

Cover Photo: Jaroslav Pachy Sr./Shutterstock Images
Interior Photos: Jaroslav Pachy Sr./Shutterstock Images, 1; iStockphoto, 4–5, 6–7, 9, 12; Johnny Habell/
Shutterstock Images, 8; People Images/iStockphoto, 11; T. Fox Foto/Shutterstock Images, 13; Roy Luck CC2.0, 14–15;
Shutterstock Images, 16, 17; Piotr Zajac/Shutterstock Images, 19; Mike Flippo/Shutterstock Images, 21

Editor: Brienna Rossiter
Series Designer: Madeline Berger
Art Direction: Dorothy Toth

**Publisher's Cataloging-in-Publication Data**
Names: Rivera, Andrea, author.
Title: Trucks / by Andrea Rivera.
Description: Minneapolis, MN : Abdo Zoom, 2017. | Series: Powerful machines |
    Includes bibliographical references and index.
Identifiers: LCCN 2016949157 | ISBN 9781680799507 (lib. bdg.) |
    ISBN 9781624025365 (ebook) | ISBN 9781624025921 (Read-to-me ebook)
Subjects: LCSH: Trucks--Juvenile literature.
Classification: DDC 629.224--dc23
LC record available at http://lccn.loc.gov/2016949157

# Table of Contents

Trucks are big vehicles.
There are many kinds of trucks.

Some pull loads.
Others carry goods.

Big trucks have many tires.
This helps them carry heavy things.

They get
power from
strong **engines**.

Garbage trucks take trash to landfills.

8

An arm picks up the trash can.
It dumps the trash into the truck.

A blade or wall crushes the trash. It makes the trash smaller. This helps the truck hold more trash.

A dump truck's bed can lift.
The driver pulls a lever.

Pressure moves a **piston**.
The piston pushes the truck's bed
up at one end. This pours the
load out the other end.

The biggest
dump truck is too
big to drive. It has to
be taken apart.

The pieces are sent to a new **construction** site. Then the truck is put back together.

# Art

In India and Pakistan, people paint fancy patterns on their trucks.

They use bright colors.

A car's engine has about 140 **horsepower**. Monster trucks are much stronger. Their engines can have 2,000 horsepower.

- Semitrucks pull trailers full of goods. A semitruck with a full trailer weighs about 80,000 pounds (36,300 kg).

- Monster trucks have huge tires. The tires are 66 inches (168 cm) tall.

- Dump trucks are the biggest kind of trucks.

- The biggest dump truck can haul almost 500 tons (450 tonnes) of goods. That is about as heavy as four blue whales!

# Glossary

**bed** - the back part of a dump truck that can carry things.

**construction** - building or making something.

**engine** - a machine that uses energy to run or move something.

**horsepower** - a measurement of how fast or strong an engine is.

**landfill** - a place where garbage is taken and buried underground.

**piston** - a short tube that moves up and down inside a bigger tube.

# Booklinks

For more information
on trucks, please visit
booklinks.abdopublishing.com

Zoom In on STEAM!

Learn even more with the Abdo Zoom
STEAM database. Check out
abdozoom.com for more information.

# Index